Live Laugh
and be Blessed

LiveLaugh
and be Blessed

finding humor
and holiness in
everyday moments

anne bryan smollin

author of *Tickle Your Soul*

SORIN BOOKS NOTRE DAME, INDIANA

Grateful acknowledgment to Canticle Press, Latham, New York, for permission to reprint the poem "The Child Who Brought Me One Small Rose" by Eileen Lomasney.

Scripture quotations are from the *New Revised Standard Version* of the Bible, copyright © 1993 and 1989 by the Division of Christian Education of the National Council of Churches of Christ in the U. S. A. Used by permission. All rights reserved.

www.sorinbooks.com

ISBN-10   1-893732-98-3
ISBN-13   978-1-893732-98-8

Cover and text design by Brian C. Conley

Printed and bound in the United States of America.

Library of Congress Cataloging-in-Publication Data is available.

THIS BOOK IS FOR
MY FAMILY AND FRIENDS—
THE BLESSINGS IN MY LIFE.

Thank you for all you are to me.

Contents

Introduction

I love giving lectures. I meet so many wonderful people. I truly believe that when we touch another's life or another touches ours we are never the same. We carry all those people in our heart forever. We are forever connected. What a grace!

I am humbled when someone speaks to me about one of my books and comments on the content of a lecture. They open their heart and confide how a certain line or a story I had told helped them see things in a different way. Sometimes I hear marvelous sharings that occur in cancer groups or in meditation groups where they are using one of my books for discussion. I am often touched by the letters I receive from people who have read a story in one of my books, and they need me to know what it did to unlock a hurt or a bitterness or challenged them to forgive another.

Truly, I do not deserve this praise. I love to tell these stories and I love to share these moments of joy and laughter. I get so much more out of it than those to whom I am speaking or for whom I am writing. I guess that's what the boomerang principle is all about. Whatever we give away always comes back. When we help others laugh, they bless us with laughter in our life. When we are kind and thoughtful toward others, we receive that gift back a hundredfold.

It's really wonderful to think that it's never too late to be happy, to be kind, to be generous, to be more fully alive. It's never too late to take time to spend a few minutes with someone we love or call someone on the telephone for no other reason than to just say "Hi" and tell them we were thinking of them. It's never too late to forgive someone and let go of some hurt. Life is short. We only really have this very moment! To live it fully is a gift we give back to ourselves.

It's not hard to find the joy in life and grasp the beauty of the moment. It's a choice we can make. And then we find ourselves lighter, more in touch, more aware, and more eager to share life with others.

People spend so much time worrying about getting old that they get old! They worry so much about not having enough money or being sick or being alone that they create that life script for themselves. There are only so many things we can control; getting older isn't one of them, but growing old is. Our health is a gift that we must be grateful for, appreciate, and do all we can to maintain. Harvard Medical School conducted a study on adult development with healthy people born in the 1920s, 1930s, and 1940s and found that attitude is the deciding factor in how we age. We mature as we age and some of our functions even improve. Because of many advance technologies we have learned to live longer, but have we learned to live well? It is not enough to just exist—to be physically alive. We must be physically, mentally, emotionally, and spiritually alive. We must live each moment. We must develop attitudes of gratitude, compassion, and reverence. We must grow to see the joy in the moment in front of us—the joy of a sunny day, or the beauty of a winter snowstorm, or the exquisite colors of a sunset, or the smile on the face of a young child, or the twinkle in an older person's eye.

All of us need to check our attitudes and monitor our reactions. What do you do if you are caught in a traffic jam and know it will result in your being late for an appointment? What do you do when someone needs just a few minutes of your time and needs to share a concern with you? What do you do when you have to change your plans because the weather prevents you from going someplace, or travel plans have changed, or an unexpected crisis occurs? How do you respond when you are waiting for someone and he is late? Or when someone shares a story with you that she has told you a million times?

If only we could learn to live each moment and find joy in it. The next time it begins to snow, put on your coat and boots and stand still for a moment and let the snow cover you. Stand in awe that no two snowflakes are the same. The next time you pass a park, pull over and sit for a moment and watch the children play. Stay there until you find yourself laughing as hard as they are. The next time you are caught in a traffic jam, decide that it is a gift to yourself. No one knows where you are. We have few private moments; when we get one we miss it. So it is my hope that you will enjoy these stories and use them to live the moment.

I have another love—photography. My camera is my stress reducer. I relax and treat myself to those healthy moments we all need when I go out with my camera and find the beauty of a flower or the story revealed in someone's eyes. My photos are special to me, and each holds a story. Some of them are included throughout the

Live, Laugh, and

book. It is my hope that you, too, will find them special, that they will speak to you, and that you will discover something beautiful in them.

My wish for all of you will always be that you live well, love much, and laugh often.

12

Laughter

TIME SPENT LAUGHING IS TIME SPENT WITH THE GODS.
—JAPANESE PROVERB

There is a wonderful story about a construction worker who brought his lunch every day to his work site.

All the men working at the project ate lunch together at break time. Each day, the construction worker opened his lunch box and said, "Bologna again." Every day the same scene was repeated: the construction worker opened his lunch box and said, "Bologna again." This went on for weeks. The other men were tired of hearing him say the same thing every day. One of them finally said to him, "If you're so tired of baloney sandwiches, why don't you ask your wife to make you something besides a bologna sandwich?" The construction worker replied, "Oh, my wife doesn't make my sandwiches. I do."

This story resonates with many of us. We sometimes feed ourselves a lot of baloney and don't do anything about it! Many stay stuck in negativity with a perspective framed in deprivation rather than abundance. For example, they choose to see the glass as half empty. Negative people are very interesting. Did you ever notice how they whine? They develop an irritating sound to their voice as they incessantly whine with such interminable phrases as:

"Nothing good ever happens to me";

"I never get picked for any committee";

and

"I'll never win the lottery."

After listening for a while you really want to say, "Get off the cross. We need the wood."

We have been blessed with the ability to make choices; these choices offer us the opportunity to see things differently and to change our behavior. We don't have to eat bologna sandwiches every day. We can let our lives be touched with the positive energy around us and see the good that is right in front of us. We can find ways to laugh and be connected to others. We can find ways to be grateful for the blessings that are granted us daily. We can change our thinking from negative to positive. We can learn to believe in ourselves and live each moment we are given more fully.

I think it would be great if we could open our spiritual lunch boxes daily and find some soul food in them. If we could find some laughter and joy we would be healthier and wiser people. If we could find some surprises and reasons to hope we would be more balanced people. The best thing about this is that we can be empowered to do this for ourselves! We can be people who make a choice to live life fully. We can be people who learn to see the joy in the moment. We can be people who surround ourselves with positive, healthy people. We can be people who feed ourselves more than bologna.

Recently, a priest friend of mine was suffering through a very stressful situation. He is a public figure and is often quoted in national papers as a spokesperson for his brother priests. We were talking about the impact of stress on those being unjustly judged in the media. Both of us were concerned about the impact that the current crisis in the church would have on the mental and physical well-being of those who were misjudged or unjustly accused. I asked him how he was dealing with it in his own personal life. Without hesitation he said, "Each day I have a *holy* hour and I have a *happy* hour!"

What wonderful balance! We all need a holy hour where we can grow in our faith. We feed our soul and stay focused and in touch with God's presence in our life. We all need a happy hour, too, where we can balance our daily stresses. Happy hours can be filled with surrounding ourselves with happy people. They can be moments in our day where we give ourselves life-giving seconds to breathe deeply in the moment, relaxing our bodies. I believe happy hours can be holy hours as well; they are the present moments when we choose to live intentionally, allowing those times to touch us in the depth of our souls. We become refreshed. Our perceptions are broadened as we see things in a new and different way, often finding ourselves to be more creative as a result.

In both holy hours and happy hours we are connected to others. It is this connection that empowers us and helps us deal with stresses and frustrations. Connections gift us with a way out of our ruts and into a creative space with new eyes and ears, empowering us to experience life beyond bologna sandwiches. The energy we feel from our connections carries us through difficult moments. This energy is like soul food. It is the nutrition that gives us

15

20/20 vision to see our world through wide eyes, including the periphery. This energy enables us to perceive all the world without blinders; it allows us to have a clearer, wider picture of our place in the human family. We can then care about the starving people in the world. Homeless people are not foreign to us. What happens in Sudan or Iraq affects us because we feel connected. The more we are connected to other people, the more we realize our connection to the whole universe. Connections take us beyond ourselves and place us in the context of the whole. We are connected to the earth and the stars. "It is your business," Horace writes, "when the wall next door catches fire."

> You—and you alone—will have stars as
>   no one else has them.
> In one of them I shall be laughing.
> And so it will be as if all the stars were
>   laughing when you look at the sky at
>   night.
> You—only you—will have stars that can
>   laugh!
> And when your sorrow is comforted
>   (time soothes all sorrows),
> You will be content that you have known
>   me.

> —ANTOINE DE SAINT-EXUPERY,
> THE LITTLE PRINCE

THEN OUR MOUTH WAS FILLED WITH LAUGHTER, AND OUR TONGUE WITH SHOUTS OF JOY; THEN IT WAS SAID AMONG THE NATIONS, "THE LORD HAS DONE GREAT THINGS FOR THEM." THE LORD HAS DONE GREAT THINGS FOR US, AND WE REJOICED.

—PSALM 126:2–3

19

Live Life Seriously

If only we could teach ourselves to live in the moment. We are always thinking about what we have to do next, or what we forgot to do, or what we wished we had done. Our minds are so fixed on things on our "to do" list that we miss the opportunity to live in the present.

There is a story about the many ways God is revealed to us:

The man whispered, "God, speak to me."
And the meadowlark sang.
But the man did not hear.
So the man yelled, "God, speak to me."
And thunder and lightning rolled across the sky.
But the man did not listen.
The man looked around and said, "God, let me see you."
And a star shone brightly.
But the man did not see.

And the man shouted, "God, show me a miracle."
And a life was born.
But the man did not notice.
So the man cried out in despair, "Touch me, God, and let me know you are here."
Whereupon God reached down and touched the man.
But the man brushed the butterfly away and walked on.

How often we miss the subtle butterfly . . . a gentle smile of an aged person, the supportive words of a friend, a gracious compliment of a coworker, or the good wishes of a colleague.

Alcoholics Anonymous (AA) is one of the most effective self-help models we have in our culture. The philosophy of AA is to live each day fully. The program encourages its members to believe in their worth and to be responsible for their behavior. It encourages a healthy dependency on a higher power and creates a supportive model for its members.

These principles are for everyone. Each of us could slow down and try to live the moment as fully as possible. We might have to start with a half day or even an hour. But the important thing is to choose to live as fully as possible. We do not have to do it alone; we can call our humor buddy. Everyone needs a humor buddy—a person who helps us laugh and helps us see the joy in the moment. What a wonderful resource! This person is like a soul mate because we grow in trust as well as vulnerability, sharing some of our most uncomfortable situations as well as our hysterically funny moments.

We find ourselves laughing more, which lifts us up. It relieves some of the stress and helps us cope with our anger and fear. Life becomes worth living. This doesn't mean that we won't have hard and difficult things to deal with in our daily lives. It doesn't mean we see the world through rose-colored glasses. It does mean we can keep a sense of balance in our life. We can see there are options and choices. We can remember that we don't have to stay stuck in negative stress. We can realize that there are other options and we can find new solutions.

Stress is a physiological response in the body. Each of us reacts with a different emotional response. It's important to learn how to de-stress ourselves. This involves changing the way we think. When something negative happens to us we can reframe the experience. Don't deny or avoid it, but admit that the situation was hurtful or upsetting. Then we must learn from the situation. Holding on to negative stress only increases the potential for more harm and sickness to affect us. Acknowledging our helplessness is also important because there are times when we cannot change a situation. Our power is in identifying the situation, changing how we think about it, and letting it go to prevent being victimized by the stress of it.

There is a story about a troubled old man. Life seemed to hand him one jolt after another, but he faced each obstacle with a smile and a cheery disposition.

An acquaintance of the man finally asked him how he managed to stay so happy despite his hardships.

23

Live, Laugh, and

The old man quickly answered: "Well, the Bible often says, 'And it came to pass,' but never once does it say, 'It came to stay.'"

Perhaps we should remember that LAUGHTER:
Lightens the load;
Avoids negativity;
Unites hearts;
Gathers people together;
Heals heartache;
Tickles the soul;
Energizes the human spirit; and
Restores us to wholeness and holiness.

CHAPTER 3

Be Willing to Be Surprised

IT IS A HAPPY TALENT TO KNOW HOW TO PLAY.
—RALPH WALDO EMERSON

I have a wonderful friend, Kathleen. We have teased her over the years because Kath begins many projects and joins many clubs but rarely lasts more than two weeks at any of them. She joined a yoga class. That lasted two weeks. She decided to ride her bicycle for exercise. She had the bicycle tuned up and bought a new helmet. That lasted two weeks. Then she joined a swim class. That lasted two weeks. Now we just listen to her when she talks about her newest interest and wisely put our money on the fact that this latest venture will last two weeks.

Once she surprised us. For twenty-two weeks, Kath was a member of Weight Watchers. She joined the diet program because she had had a year filled with many unhappy losses and decided she wanted to even out her life with some promising gains. She had heard that the Weight Watchers program could offer her balance and encouragement. I was very supportive to her throughout those weeks. I called her and inquired about how she was doing. When I saw her I praised her accomplishments. I tried to acknowledge her successes and tried to display a great interest in her attempts to bring balance into her life.

Live, Laugh, and

About sixteen weeks into the program, Kath called one Saturday afternoon and asked me to go for a walk. That was probably the last thing I would have chosen to do that day. The previous week was very full with commitments and I was so looking forward to sitting in my comfortable chair just reading my novel. I didn't want to do anything.

When I told Kath I really didn't want to go for a walk but just wanted to sit still, she began reciting a list of reasons that were intended for me to change my mind.

"You always tell others they have to choose to be healthy."

"You never do any exercise."

"You need to practice what you preach."

Then she mapped out the route we would take for this walk. At the end of the walk we would pass an ice-cream shop where we could go in and get a small ice-cream cone! That was my reward; it was the carrot she used to motivate me.

All right! I gave in. She picked me up and we began our adventure. People who are regular walkers are like cult members! They have rules: there is a defined way to walk and you must swing your arms as you do it. Additionally, you're supposed to maintain a brisk pace and the emphasis is on walking, not talking. I was failing miserably. I wasn't walking briskly, nor was I swinging my arms correctly; I was telling her stories and we were laughing hysterically. She reminded me that this was not the purpose of our walk. Finally we arrived at the ice-cream shop. My reward awaited me. I quickly entered the store and ordered my small ice-cream cone. Now, have you ever had a *small* ice-cream cone? It is comparable to a fleeting memory. You can have the cone finished before you even leave the store!

The following week she called again on Saturday afternoon and informed me she was coming over to get me so we could go for "our" walk.

"*Our* walk!" Where did that phrase originate? I never put those words together. Again she told me the route and promised me that we would stop for our small ice-cream cone when we got to the end of the path. Deciding I had managed to survive the previous week's adventure, I gave in and agreed to go for another walk with my friend.

This time it was a disaster! Not only did I not walk briskly or swing my arms correctly, but this time we met several people we knew as we walked along the path. I stopped and talked to each one and spent several minutes sharing stories. Kath reminded me that this was not acceptable behavior. You don't stop and talk to people; you keep walking. I really didn't know this because I am not a walker!

27

As we approached the ice-cream shop, my eyes drifted over to a car parked near the doorway. The bumper sticker on the back of the car read: *Fat people are harder to kidnap.* I stopped my friend and pointed to the bumper sticker. I then decided I needed to take care of myself. So, I went into the store and got the largest ice-cream cone they could make.

If only we could look for the surprises in our lives: the smiles on people's faces, the funny stories people tell, the bumper stickers on cars, the billboards on highways, the surprise phone calls we receive, the snail mail note someone took time to write.

Surprises help us smile. They are spontaneous and catch us off guard. They disarm us and stop us in the moment. Surprises can help us deal with the reality in front of us. They encourage us not to take ourselves so seriously.

Given the choice, people would choose truly living over just surviving. We want to have surprises and moments when we laugh our insides out. We want memories that bring a smile to our face and warmth to our hearts on a cold day.

A famous motivational guru was conducting a seminar for a large number of participants. The leader asked for three of the participants to volunteer and invited them up on the stage. He asked them to introduce themselves to the audience and explain what line of work they were in. There was a lawyer, a nurse, and a mechanic. He then asked each of them the same question:

"When you die and people are standing in front of your coffin, what do you hope they'll say?"

The lawyer said, "I hope people will remember I was a fair and just lawyer. I hope my clients will say I was an honest lawyer."

The nurse was also a mother, and she replied, "I hope my children and my patients will remember me as caring and warm and nurturing and compassionate. I hope they will remember I attended to their needs."

The mechanic said, "If I was dead and my friends were standing by the casket I hope I would hear someone say, 'I think I see him breathing.'"

We all want to live. *How* we live is our choice. Some people choose to experience life as one negative event after another. Others will fondly recall life-giving and energizing occasions more frequently than hard times. Focusing on that positive energy helps us keep our days in balance. And most of the time these moments have an element of surprise.

29

THIS IS THE DAY THAT THE LORD HAS MADE; LET US

REJOICE AND BE GLAD IN IT.

—PSALM 118:24

30

CHAPTER 4

Expect the Unexpected

THE SOUL SHOULD ALWAYS STAND AJAR,
READY TO WELCOME THE ECSTATIC EXPERIENCE.
—EMILY DICKINSON

I once heard a priest in the Albany Diocese tell a story he claimed to be true. Apparently, years ago there was a process that the newly ordained priests were expected to follow. They had to meet with the bishop of the diocese each year and had to pass a theological exam. No one ever knew what would be asked, so this created a lot of anxiety and fear.

Two newly ordained men were driving together to meet the bishop. One of the priests was very smart and, for many, the hope and future of the diocese. The other was a rather ordinary guy who struggled with academic studies. The latter was very fearful and tense about this meeting.

While driving to the bishop's office, the less academic priest kept verbalizing his fear and frustration. The smarter priest tried very hard to relax his companion but couldn't find answers. Finally, the brilliant cleric came up with a solution.

"I'll go into the bishop's office first and I'll leave the door ajar. You stand close to the door and listen. When the bishop asks me the question, I will try to speak loud enough for you to be able to hear my response. Then when you go in you will know the answer."

The other priest tried to relax. He trusted his friend and knew he wanted to help him out.

As the smarter priest went into the bishop's office he was careful to leave the door open a bit. The bishop greeted him warmly. He loved this man and was so proud he was a priest in the diocese. The bishop wasted no time. "My son," he said, "tell me, what would you do if you were celebrating Mass and had just finished consecrating the wine and a mosquito landed in the cup?"

Without hesitating, the priest said, "Your Excellency, I would do one of two things. I would either consume it or I would take it out, put it between my fingers, carry it outside, and dispose of it appropriately."

"Of course," beamed the bishop. "As it is said, you are the most intelligent young man we have. You are a gift to our diocese. You will certainly lead us and bring many blessings to our diocese."

The young priest quickly said, "Oh no, Bishop. With your outstanding leadership and having you as such a marvelous role model, I only hope I can follow in your footsteps."

Now it was time for the other priest to enter. The bishop wasted no time in getting down to the business at hand. "My son, tell me. What would you do if, while you were celebrating Mass, a cow came into the church and walked over to the holy water font and began drinking from it?"

Without hesitating the priest said, "Your Excellency, I would do one of two things. I would either consume it or I would take it out, put it between my fingers, carry it outside, and dispose of it correctly."

The bishop responded angrily, "What they say about you is correct. You are not at all intelligent. There is no hope for you. You are a disgrace to the diocese."

The priest said, "Oh no, Bishop. With your outstanding leadership and having you as such a marvelous role model, I can only hope to follow in your footsteps."

Listening isn't always one of our gifts. Preoccupied with preparing a response, we are thinking ahead, anticipating what someone is going to say. We have answers ready and sometimes we miss the questions. Sometimes we even miss the answers. At times it is like we speak a different language. Parents often feel this way when speaking to their children. Adolescents go through a period in their life when they march to a different drummer.

A businesswoman was driving toward home in Arizona. Ahead of her she saw an old Native-American woman walking through the desert with bowls on her head. The businesswoman pulled the car over and invited the woman to ride with her for a while. Seeing the bag on the passenger seat, the driver apologized, "Don't worry about that. Just put the bag on the floor. It's a silver necklace I got for my husband." The old woman was quiet for a moment, and then said, thoughtfully, "Good trade."

Perhaps we need to listen with new ears, with our inner ear to hear the voices around us and the humor that is in our daily lives. Perhaps we need to keep a "joy journal" so that we can record daily moments that bring laughter to our life. The scenes and words that bring smiles to our faces are such valuable entries for this journal. When we keep such a journal and record in it daily, we train ourselves to see the things that are filled with joy and laughter. We begin looking for things in our day that we can record. What a valuable resource we would have and how much healthier a perspective we would bring into our daily life.

Laughter and joy help us relax by loosening up some of the tension in our body. Laughter has a positive effect on the immune system. It helps us cope with daily stress. We can then enjoy people more and even hear what they are saying and asking.

All of us have at one time or another experienced a closed mind—we already have something set in our mind. We can't see outside the box!

I recently gave a lecture at West Point, New York. Since 9/11, the security has been very tight. Arriving on the property, I was stopped at a checkpoint and asked where I was going. I immediately took out my letter of confirmation and pointed to "Hotel Thayer." I was told to take the first right and the hotel was at the top of the hill. I would then have to drive down the hill to another checkpoint which would lead into the parking lot.

As I stopped at the second checkpoint, a cadet armed with a machine gun approached my car. At the same time another cadet walked to the front of the car, preventing me from driving through. The fellow on the driver's side said, "Open your hood and your trunk, ma'am."

Surprised and wondering, I said, "Pardon me?"

"Open your hood and your trunk, ma'am," he repeated.

I then began to explain that I could open the trunk with my key, but the hood opened from the front. He repeated, "Open your hood and your trunk, ma'am."

I tried to explain, "Sir, you don't understand. This is a poverty car. It doesn't even have power windows. It has nothing. I can open the trunk but you have to open the hood from the front of the car."

Without blinking he said, "Open your hood and your trunk ma'am." At this request I was surrounded by two other machine-gun-armed cadets. Now I was thinking that I was going to be shot all because the sister who buys our cars is so cheap.

I continued to explain, "Sir, I am a Sister of Saint Joseph and the sister who buys cars for the community is so cheap that she doesn't put any extras in the cars. If we had to pay extra for brakes we wouldn't have them."

37

"Open your hood and your trunk, ma'am," he repeated, not changing either his expression or his request.

"Sir, I can't."

The cadet finally looked at me and said, "Would you mind if I tried?"

"Of course not."

He then opened the car door, reached under the dash, pulled a lever, and the hood popped up.

There were no more questions. I think he thought I was probably too dumb to have a bomb or any other weapon hidden. He just told me to drive into the parking lot.

How often we can't hear because our opinions are already formed. We've made up our mind and we stay stuck in that repeated tape playing in our mind. Thinking creatively, finding a new idea, a different perspective—all of those are foreign to us. What's worse, it is times like these that we close our eyes and ears to any possibilities.

Sometimes we just don't hear what another person is asking. We've already decided what they are saying.

There's a story of a man who went out to a restaurant for dinner. He called the waiter over and said, "I can't eat this soup."

The waiter replied, "I am sorry sir, I'll call the manager."

When the manager came over to the table the guest said, "Mr. Manager, I can't eat this soup."

The manager replied, "I will call the chef."

When the chef came over to the table, the diner said, "Chef, I can't eat this soup."

The chef said, "What's wrong with it?"

The diner replied, "Nothing. I just don't have a spoon."

If we could relax and be present to the moment in front of us we would live life a bit lighter. We would find ways to accept what is before us. We would be gifted with the humor and joy of so many of our ordinary moments.

Often when our ears are blocked, we let our fears define the moment. Then we become paralyzed. We lose our freedom to live the moment fully by thinking beyond that present moment.

CHAPTER 5

Be Happy . . . Be Grateful

GREATNESS IS MAKING OTHERS FEEL GREAT!
—G. K. CHESTERTON

People of gratitude are people who create joy and are more likely to help others. People who can thank others and recognize goodness are healthier people and are more optimistic. They also have less stress in their life. A simple thing like being aware of another's kindness and seeing the blessings in one's life enhances our life; we become more positive.

Wouldn't we live in a wonderful world if people spent more time thanking people and expressing gratitude rather than being negative, sarcastic, and rude to each other? Wouldn't that increase our desire to want to spend more time with these people? Wouldn't we have more fun?

My mother is an outstanding woman. She is always thinking of others and probably has given more rides to people, provided more lunches, and contributed to more charitable organizations than hundreds of people. My mother loves shoes and coats. All of her life she has had a soft spot in her heart for these things. We tease her that she always needs a pair of shoes for every outfit.

Mom had just purchased a new winter coat. It was lovely. The coat was her favorite color and was most attractive. It had a soft fur collar that made it special. My sister and I were sitting at the dining room table with her soon after she bought the coat, when she began a conversation with a sentence that could have been missed if one was not listening. "I really need a new winter coat."

I glanced at my sister. Both of us knew she had gotten a coat just two weeks before. I looked back at my mother. I asked, "Mom, what happened to your new coat?" She told us about a woman who had stopped in to see her during the week. It was very cold. It was snowing heavily and as my mother and the woman shared a cup of coffee, my mother realized her friend had only a thin coat. So my mother went into her closet and gave her the new coat. I said, "Mom, you have loads of coats. Why did you give her your brand new coat?"

My mother quietly said, "Aren't we supposed to give the best of what we have?"

Now, how does one argue with that? My mother reminded us of how much we have. We need to be grateful for all of it. It is our responsibility to share with those who are not as richly blessed.

I wonder what we could give away every day? How about some smiles? How about some kind words or some compliments? The more we say "thank you" the more we begin to see all the things for which we can be thankful.

It is really wonderful how we end up getting back whatever we give away. It's that old boomerang principle: "Whatever you give away always comes back."

I was recently asked to give the College of Saint Rose graduation address. People always say they never remember what was said at their graduation. Some don't even remember the person who gave the address. But a few remember the words or the message, so I decided that I was going to give the best graduation address ever. I was going to stand in front of the graduates and throw out a boomerang. When it came back I was simply going to say, "Remember, whatever you give away always comes back." And then I was going to sit down. I figured everyone would remember that graduation address.

I eagerly shared my idea with the sister with whom I live, and she quickly told me I could not do it. "Boomerangs can be lethal weapons. You'll take someone's head off if you don't know what you're doing. We'll be sued."

Even though I had to abandon my idea, I am practicing. I know I will be asked to give another graduation address someday and I'm going to throw that boomerang.

43

It is so true. We get back so much more than we give. For example, when we smile at someone we receive more smiles in return; when we compliment a person we receive back a hundredfold.

By counting our blessings we become more aware of them. As we look daily at our life and see how blessed we are, we begin to see the goodness in others—how people reach out and touch lives in a positive way. I wonder, if we fall asleep counting our blessings, would we have a better night's sleep? I wonder if we could reduce physical pain or cut down on aggression and conflict by focusing more on abundance—encouraging goodness, not guns; acknowledging blessings, not bullying?

Counting our blessings might afford us less anxiety, with the possibility of shrinking our fears. Counting our blessings would tune us in to the laughter and joy that occurs in everyday life. We would be more fun to be around. That, in turn, would decrease the loneliness and isolation people feel. We would want to bond with positive people who help us feel better and appreciate us. We would be healthier because we would be laughing more and enjoying life. We would appreciate little things in our life like flowers, sunrises, changing leaves, and the beauty of the first snowfall. We would feel appreciated and would then want to contribute more, work harder, and do our part in any project we are involved in. We wouldn't find ourselves so busy that we wouldn't have time to play with a young child or sing a silly song with another. We would take the time to joke with others and listen to their stories. If we could do that in our backyard we could take it to our city, our country, and the broader world.

I had the privilege of being invited to the New York State Governor's Prayer Breakfast one year. It was a very impressive breakfast with people of all walks of life represented: politicians, religious leaders, state workers, CEOs, doctors, lawyers, to name a few. The guest speaker was Eileen Collins, the first woman space commander. She was fantastic. Humbly, she stood before this gathering of 1,200 people. She said she didn't feel that she had the expertise to speak to this crowd about prayer. Was she ever wrong! Instead, she took the approach of talking about the role of prayer in her personal life. She talked about growing up in a Catholic household and attending Catholic schools and the influence this had on her life. She talked about meeting the man she would marry and discussing, before marriage, what role God would have in their life. She shared the story of a difficult pregnancy that eventually resulted in a beautiful, healthy daughter. Finally, she recalled being in outer space and looking down to earth. She saw the mountain where Muhammad walked. She looked at the Sea of Galilee and thought of Jesus. Eileen said that from outer space there are no differences—no political, racial, ethnic, social, or religious differences. She saw one big world that needed to work together.

45

Maybe we would have that world working together if we were people who expressed gratitude and affirmation to each other. Maybe we would be in a peaceful environment if we would walk next to one another, honoring differences and respecting diversity, finding that our common ground enables us to laugh together and share life with one another. There is a wonderful Yiddish proverb:

> If you cannot be grateful for what you
> have received, then be thankful for what
> you have been spared.

THE VERY FIRST WORD THE ANGEL GABRIEL SAID TO MARY WAS "REJOICE."

"REJOICE, YOU WHO ENJOY GOD'S FAVOR! THE LORD IS WITH YOU."

—LUKE 1:28 (NJB)

Chapter 6

Life Is Not a Bowl of Cherries or a Stack of Pits

ALL OF US ARE RESPONSIBLE FOR ONE ANOTHER.
—Talmud

Life is not a bowl of cherries. Even making our best efforts to see positively and act proactively in order to live a balanced life, we will be confronted with hurts, disappointments, and scattered dreams. All of us have experienced the loss of a loved one, the betrayal of a friend, the frustration of a failed endeavor, and the disappointment of things not going as expected. Even though we know (in our heads) that we will experience loss and sadness, most of us are not prepared to deal with the situation when we are going through it (in our hearts). The biggest distance in the world can be from our hearts to our heads! Loss, betrayal, sadness, or disappointment can leave us helpless and feeling alone.

I was unjustly accused of something and the whole incident turned my life upside down. A dark cloud hung over my head and never left me. I would get up in the morning and immediately get the newspaper. Searching through the "Capital Region" section, I would look to see if my name was in the paper that day and what was now being said about me. When I got to the obituaries, I was grateful not to read my name and know I was cleared for that day at least.

It is disheartening to read negative words about yourself and what you're accused of allegedly saying or doing. The frustrating part is to know that you cannot respond because of legal proceedings and ethical conduct. You cannot make statements; you cannot correct accusations. You can only hope that the people who know you, love you, and believe in you will see through the untruths that are being written. Life seems to go on for everyone. But when you are persecuted unjustly, everything you believe to be true about good triumphing over evil is shaken, and you wonder if there really is a light at the end of the tunnel.

So many times I said a prayer in thanksgiving that there was no truth to those statements being publicly made about me. I did not need to apologize to anyone. I did not regret a decision or wish I had made another choice. I could feel confident in personal integrity and professional conduct. Nevertheless, it did not take away from the fact that I felt like the character in *The Scarlet Letter,* imprinted with a big red letter that marked my sin for the whole world to see. Daily I thanked God for my family, friends, and community members who supported me through their thoughts, cards, prayers, and messages of encouragement, believing that truth would prevail and I would be exonerated.

Healing does take place in time, but it is impossible to believe in that process and feel relief while going through the pain. Yet it is in the encouraging smiles, comforting words, joyful laughter, and warm hugs freely given that life is restored to health and wholeness. They are the medicines that heal. Amazing healing takes place when human caring is evidenced and felt. Exemplifying Proverbs 17:22, "A cheerful heart is a good medicine, but a downcast spirit dries up the bones," these medicines create stronger and more whole people.

In times of trouble, we must be like the Chinese, who see crisis as opportunity. We have to look beyond the pain and see the life-giving moments as blessings. We need to be open to the affirmations that people offer us and hear their messages. We need to be responsible for ourselves and keep a sense of balance. We need to attend to the physical, mental, emotional, and spiritual aspects of our life. Our strength is in the balance. A Chinese proverb reminds us:

> You cannot prevent the birds of sorrow
> from flying over your head, but you can
> prevent them from building nests in your
> hair.

A life of joy is not a bowl of cherries. It does not offer us perpetual highs. It doesn't mean we never suffer or have difficult moments we must live through. Rather than an unrealistic Pollyannaish perspective, a life of joy is filled with trials and tribulations as well as joy and jubilation. One experiences delight and laughter as well as pain and tears. We must connect to others in either case. Joys and laughter are meant to be shared. We give each other energy and hope. We lighten each other's burdens. But pain and tears also need to be shared. They, too, enable us to connect to others. Pain and tears allow us to show others we need them. This vulnerability invites others to share our burdens. It's not easy for us to admit we need another. Our culture has put such emphasis on individuality and independence that some view it as a weakness to be dependent on another. Yet it is the very balance of

51

independence and dependence that creates the healthy interdependence. When one of us is in pain, we are all in pain. When one hurts, we all hurt. When there are tears, no eyes are dry.

When we've been hurt it is sometimes hard to let go and forgive. We know that forgiveness is not a feeling. It is an action. We can choose to forgive. Forgiveness takes time; it does not mean forgetting. A Persian proverb states: "He who wants a rose must respect the thorn." No one and no thing is perfect. Accepting that is not as easy as it may sound. Ralph Waldo Emerson reminds us:

> Finish each day and be done with it. You
> have done what you could; some blun-
> ders and absurdities no doubt crept in.
> Forget them as soon as you can.
> Tomorrow is a new day, you shall begin
> it well and serenely.

Life is a challenging process where we go from strength to strength. We grow stronger as we deal with the difficult moments in our lives. An Indian proverb teaches, "The one who has mounted an elephant will not fear the bark of a dog."

THIS DAY IS HOLY TO THE **LORD** YOUR GOD; DO NOT MOURN OR WEEP. . . . FOR THIS DAY IS HOLY TO OUR **LORD**; AND DO NOT BE GRIEVED, FOR THE JOY OF THE **LORD** IS YOUR STRENGTH.

—NEHEMIAH 8:9–10

CHAPTER 7

Half Full or Half Empty

Some people love to be negative. They love to complain and even love hearing themselves complain. If there were a bouquet of flowers that was perfectly arranged in front of them, they would see the wilted daisy. These are the people with whom we don't want to spend a lot of time. We don't need to drag ourselves down by their negativity. Not only is it unhealthy to our physical well-being but to our mental, psychological, and spiritual health as well.

Sometimes we all have to teach ourselves to be content with what is. To be content with "enough," to be satisfied with the gifts in front of us takes a while to grow into and develops with maturity and self-knowledge. Nasrudin, the archetypal wise fool, teaches us this lesson so well.

Nasrudin decided to start a flower garden. He prepared the soil and planted the seeds of many beautiful flowers. As the flowers grew, his garden was not just filled with the desired flowers, but it was also overrun by dandelions. He sought advice from gardeners all over and tried every method known to get rid of the pesky weeds, but to no avail. Finally he found his way to the sheik's palace to speak to the royal gardener. The wise old man had counseled many gardeners and suggested a variety of remedies to eliminate the dandelions. However, Nasrudin had tried all of the master gardener's suggestions. They sat together in silence for some time and finally the gardener looked at Nasrudin and said, "Well then, I suggest you learn to love dandelions."

What peace of mind comes from that choice. What a freedom!

How can we learn to accept things rather than wanting them to be different? How often do we waste away days wishing otherwise? Nothing is ever quite right or something is always missing or lacking.

Did you ever have a day that started with a problem which just snowballed into a crisis day? Those are usually the days we remember long after and even laugh about for a long time.

It was a snowy, icy day in Albany, New York, and my day was beginning with an 8:00 a.m. meeting for the College of Saint Rose. Since I only live about four minutes from the college, I waited until the last possible moment to leave the house. Our driveway is quite steep and as I cautiously began walking down the driveway to get to my car, my feet slipped from under me and I slid down the driveway. Immediately I stood up and began looking around to see if anyone had seen me. No one seemed to be looking out their front windows.

Our next-door neighbor came running out and was laughing so hard she almost fell down her own driveway. She said I looked like I was in the Olympic luge run! I noticed I had skinned my knee and ripped my stockings, but I had no time to change them. I had to get to the board meeting. After the meeting I was taping a television program on stress. Since this meeting usually lasted for one hour, I knew I had time to return home and change my stockings before traveling to the television studio.

However, as badly as the day had begun, it continued in the same vein! The board meeting went overtime and when I left the college I had no alternative but to drive directly to the television studio. Walking into the studio, I asked if we could sit behind a desk or table. This would at least hide my skinned knee and torn stocking. Unfortunately, the studio was set up and we had no time to rearrange the setting. As the program began, I tried to pull my skirt down far enough to cover my skinned knee and torn stockings. The topic was stress, its causes and how we can manage it.

The studio setting is a small room atmosphere appropriately filled with comfortable furniture. One wall of the studio has a window that overlooks the street. Cars drive by, people walk by, and some folks stop and watch the show. All of a sudden we became aware of a homeless man with his face pushed against the glass window. He began to pound on the glass and the interviewer became very distracted and anxious. Wiggling in her chair, the interviewer raised her voice and began talking faster. The homeless man continued to pound on the glass. Finally, several men, including Schenectady's mayor who was to follow me on the television program, ran out of the station. The homeless man took off. Now, a line of men could be seen running past the glass window! The interviewer concluded my segment of the program and invited the mayor to join her, unaware that the mayor had just run past the window. When he did not appear, she suggested that I stay on the set to continue. All of this had occurred on live television. The taped interview was to be replayed several other times. I later suggested that the tape be used to demonstrate how to reduce stress. It seemed like a teachable moment to me!

People who saw the show asked if we had staged the scene to be able to show how one can deal with stress. I assured them it was extremely spontaneous. And no one even noticed my knee or my stocking.

Accepting situations as they are and making the best of them not only helps us keep our stress level down, but also we begin to see the glass as half full. The negative reaction is not what we choose.

It is possible to learn to tune in to the humor that is right in front of us.

There was an elderly woman who had been hard of hearing for years. Her family and friends were always encouraging her to get a hearing aid. Finally, she gave in. After having the hearing aid for three weeks she returned to the audiologist for a minor adjustment. He said, "Your friends and relatives must be very pleased that you can hear so well now."

"Oh, I haven't told them," the woman replied. "I just sit around and listen. And you know what? I've changed my will three times!"

People say funny things. Children have the gift of saying things that make us laugh. Only when we begin to listen do we really hear. I am convinced that Robin Williams and Bill Cosby and other comedians are not any funnier than the rest of us. They have just taught themselves to be in tune with the moment, and they hear and see the funny things that are right in front of them. We can do the same.

An old French proverb advises, "The most completely lost of all days is the one in which we have not laughed." What a wasted day! Laughter improves everything— imagination, creativity, relationships, and circulation, just to name a few. Laughing makes life more enjoyable and possible to live longer, healthier, and happier.

Laughter helps us feel better. It suspends worries and problems. Laughter is a gift we can give to others. People begin to feel good about themselves. It can also help them see their problems with a different perspective. We have all experienced tension being reduced in our bodies when we laugh. When our bodies are tense and our minds are closed (as well as our eyes and ears), laughter is the medicine that relaxes us and offers a dose of positive self-esteem. We feel more self-assured and self-confident when we laugh; we feel better physically and mentally.

61

One of the greatest benefits of laughter is that we get an aerobic workout, one that doesn't require a membership to a club or the purchase of special clothes. Laughter enhances respiration and increases the amount of oxygen in the blood. The diaphragm—the large muscle that separates the chest cavity from the abdominal cavity—is used when we laugh. When we laugh, the movement of the diaphragm stimulates the stomach, kidneys, and liver, acting like an internal massage.

Research indicates that our bodies contain natural substances, such as endorphins and encephalons, that help free us of pain and illness. Stress disrupts and slows the glandular secretions of these chemicals. It also restricts blood vessels. But laughter prompts the brain to block the manufacture of immune suppressors like epinephrine and cortisone and speed up the production of immune enhancers such as beta-endorphins. These endorphins are 200 times more powerful than heroin!

John Morreall, a philosopher at the University of South Florida in Tampa, suggests that the first human laughter may have begun as a gesture of shared relief at the passing of some danger. He suggested, "It's a signal that now we can relax." Muscles relax throughout the body when a person is laughing. People have experienced laughing so hard that they have to hold onto something to prevent themselves from falling over. Laughter may be a signal of trust in one's companions.

Laughter helps strengthen social bonds. We always feel safer with people we laugh with; they give us a sense of security and safety. According to Mahadev Apte, a cultural anthropologist at Duke University in Durham, North Carolina, "Laughter occurs when people are comfortable with one another, when they feel open and free. And the more laughter, the more bonding within the group." It has been proven that people laugh louder and longer when in larger groups. Willibald Ruch, a psychologist at the University of Dusseldorf, says that even nitrous oxide, or laughing gas, loses much of its potency if taken in solitude. Plato told us, "You can discover more about a person in an hour of play than in a year of conversation."

We worry that we won't be responsible if we play too much. We need to create a stern exterior so we will be taken seriously! How dull! "Unless you become like little children. . . ." Perhaps we are never supposed to lose the spontaneity and healthy freedom of little children. We watch them play and often see them entertain themselves with empty boxes or spoons or pans. They can spend hours in a pile of dirt or just observing an ant hill. When children laugh, their whole body gives evidence of that moment. Every muscle is activated. Their laughter and joy are contagious. Job reminds us, "God fills our mouths with laughter."

63

Some people need to develop the ability to laugh at themselves. Being able to laugh at ourselves can be a sign of a maturing spirituality, rooted in the gifts of light-heartedness, humor, and joy.

Mother Teresa and Dorothy Day emphasized the importance of the spirit of joy in ministering to the poor and suffering. St. Teresa of Avila prayed, "From serious, sullen saints, save us, O Lord." Jesus promised to bring laughter to those who were poor, downtrodden, sick, prisoners, and oppressed, and predicted that those who weep now shall know laughter in the kingdom of God.

So laughing and being in the company of those with whom we can laugh is really a life-giving experience. It is a holy moment when we laugh. It is a communion experience. The Qur'an states, "They deserve paradise who make their companions laugh." The ability to laugh and enjoy life is a measure of our psychological and spiritual well-being.

Chapter 8

Choices

SLOW DOWN AND ENJOY LIFE.
IT'S NOT THE SCENERY YOU MISS BY GOING TOO FAST—YOU ALSO MISS THE
SENSE OF WHERE YOU ARE GOING AND WHY.
—EDDIE CANTOR

Sometimes we get comfortable with repetition and ritual. Instead of keeping a passion in our life, we tend to settle for "same old, same old." With disbelief, we wonder why we feel bored. In the worst-case scenario, this could lead to depression. Living life fully and finding life in the moment bless us with energy, humor, and creativity. How sad not to opt to be fully alive! Michelangelo stated, "The greatest danger for most of us is not that our aim is too high and we miss it but that it is too low and we reach it."

Fleas are trained by putting them in a cardboard box with a top on it. The fleas will jump up and hit the top of the cardboard box over and over again. But the fleas adjust their jump so that as they continue jumping, they no longer jump high enough to hit the top. When the lid is taken off the box, the fleas continue to jump but they will not jump out of the box. They have conditioned themselves to jump just high enough.

We condition ourselves, too. We believe we can only do certain things and limit our belief in ourselves. We put a lid on our behavior so often that when other opportunities or challenges present themselves, we just close our eyes and stay where we are. Instead of growing by stretching ourselves through challenges, we are content to just stay where we are.

There's a wonderful Italian proverb: "You never climb higher than the ladder you select." We settle for so little at times. We live our fears and hence we don't take risks, try new adventures, think outside the box, or learn new things about ourselves. All we need is present in the moment. In this moment is vision, health, creativity, awareness, risk, and humor. So many graces wrapped in the now.

A Native-American grandfather shared his wisdom with his grandson. He told the grandson that we have two wolves inside us who struggle with each other. One is the wolf of peace, love, and kindness. The other is the wolf of fear, greed, and hatred.

"Which wolf will win, Grandfather?"

The wise man responded, "Whichever one I feed."

We make our own choices. Those choices decide where our actions will take us. The wolf of peace, love, and kindness gifts all we meet with joy, happiness, and laughter. The wolf of fear, greed, and hatred bestows gifts of separation, alienation, and powerlessness. It really is up to us to nurture our heart and soul with peace, love, and kindness.

All of us like to be around people who hold these values and treat others with dignity. We like being around people who are pleasant and cheerful. Joyful people help create a healthy, inclusive environment. There is a sense of support one feels that creates a positive feeling. People who give peace, love, and kindness give hope to others. They're the ones we turn to when we are hurting or when there is a crisis in our life. They are the healers, inspirers, and motivators.

Those giving gifts of fear, greed, and hatred are those who drag us down. They are people who drain us. They are always unavailable and never perceive the needs of others. They only see their own reflection in the mirror and never take time to look at the faces and eyes of others. Nothing is ever more important than their agenda. No one is ever busier or more important than themselves. These sad people miss so much of life. They don't see the giftedness of others; they miss the positive. We must remember that we shape our attitudes. We can't control an event or a situation, but we can decide how we will respond to it through our attitudes.

67

A story is told of a young and ambitious rabbi who had moved into the town of a famous master. Finding no interested students, he decided to challenge the old master in public, thereby winning some followers. He caught a bird and, with it hidden in his hand, strode up to the old master, who was surrounded by students.

"If you are so great," he asked the master, "tell me if the bird is dead or alive." His plan was this: If the old master said the bird was dead, he would release it to fly away. If the master said it was alive, he would quickly crush it and then open his hand showing the dead bird. Either way, the old master would be embarrassed and lose students.

So there he stood, confronting the old master in the presence of the students. "Is the bird in my hand dead or alive?" he asked again. The master sat quietly, then replied, "Really, my friend, it's up to you."

And it is up to us! We decide, we choose, we determine our choices. We decide if we are happy. There is probably no better way to break down barriers between people than to have them laugh together. Victor Borge said, "A smile is the closest distance between two people."

Laughter brings us firmly with the present moment. It's not possible to focus on past regret or future anxiety when we're laughing. There is only the present time.

When we live the present reality we often experience new insights or have a new understanding. Our perception is broader. Sometimes we even see the obvious!

There is a story about a man who crossed the border with his donkey. He was searched to make sure he was not smuggling anything and then released. The next day the same man came across the border with his donkey. Suspicious that the man might be trying to smuggle something, since he had just crossed the border the day before, the guards performed a more thorough search. Not finding anything, they released the man again and he went on his way. Every day for two years the man arrived at the border with his donkey. Each day the guards became more and more suspicious that he was smuggling something, but each day's search revealed nothing, so they let him go.

Years later, after the man no longer crossed the border, one of the retired guards spotted the man at the market.

"Tell me," he said, "we know you were bringing something illegally across the border, but we could never find it. What was it you were smuggling?"

"Since you are retired and can't arrest me, I'll tell you. It was the donkeys."

69

"WHAT DO YOU THINK? IF A SHEPHERD HAS A HUNDRED SHEEP, AND ONE OF THEM HAS GONE ASTRAY, DOES HE NOT LEAVE THE NINETY-NINE ON THE MOUNTAINS AND GO IN SEARCH OF THE ONE THAT WENT ASTRAY? AND IF HE FINDS IT, TRULY I TELL YOU, HE REJOICES OVER IT MORE THAN OVER THE NINETY-NINE THAT NEVER WENT ASTRAY."

—MATTHEW 18:12–13

CHAPTER 9

Connected

SHARED JOYS RATHER THAN SHARED SUFFERINGS MAKE A FRIEND.
— FRIEDRICH NIETZSCHE

Being in the company of another person is a powerful experience and gift. Researchers report that when teams of people are working together on a problem, the groups that laugh most readily and most often are more creative and productive than their more dour and decorous counterparts. Playfulness is a creative state.

Researchers found that eating with one other person increased the size of each diner's meal by 28 percent. Two extra diners increased everyone's meal size by 41 percent, and six or more dinner partners led each to consume 76 percent more food. Eating with a group may cause people to linger and eat more than they would if they were alone.

The power of being with others often goes unnoticed. Margaret Mead said, "Don't think that a small group of awakened individuals cannot change the world. Indeed, it is the only thing that ever has." We can do so much when we experience a healthy interdependence with each other. Wimbledon tennis champion Althea Gibson said, "No matter what accomplishments you achieve, somebody helped you."

It is sad to see how many people choose not to interact with others or think they can do it all alone. Each of us touches another person's life and ours is, in turn, touched.

There is a story of a person who never saw how his actions and behavior would have an effect on another.

Once there was a group of people in a boat. Suddenly, one person took out a drill and started to make a hole underneath his seat. The water began to come into the boat.

The others admonished him, "What are you doing? You will sink the boat!"

The man replied, "What concern is it of yours? I am only drilling under my seat."

There are others who gift us with the awareness that others play an important part in their lives. Needing others and sharing life moments with another opens our hearts and enriches our lives.

74

Once there were two little girls who were best friends. One was Christian and the other was Jewish. After Christmas, the grandfather of the Christian girl asked her, "What did your best friend get for Christmas?"

The granddaughter thought for a moment and responded, "Oh, she's not Christmas, Grandpa; she's Hanukkah." A moment later a huge smile came across her face and she said, "But we're both Thanksgiving."

There is an Irish proverb that says, "It is in the shelter of each other that the people live." It is in our casual encounters with others that we grow. We share stories and dreams and become communion for each other. Perhaps that is the meaning of "Give us this day our daily bread."

Rabbi Hillel, in the twelfth century, wrote: "If I am not for myself, who will be for me? If I am not for others, who am I? And if not now, when?"

Interacting, talking, sharing, listening, and laughing with other people bring balance into our lives. It is essential to our development that we learn to "be" with others and that we love someone besides ourselves. The French have a saying: "What? No star, and you are going out to sea? Marching, and you have no music? Traveling, and you have no book? No love, and you are going out to live?"

Research has taught us that business leaders who achieve the best results get people to laugh three times more often than do mediocre leaders. When people laugh they are relaxed. Enjoying what they do, they are more likely to be focused, productive, and creative. They are not caught up in anger, fear, and anxiety.

People who have lots of friends, relatives, and other social ties tend to live a longer, healthier life. Just talking on the phone or getting together with friends, neighbors, or relatives improves social skills. Research is finding that the more socially engaged we are, the lower the level of cognitive impairment and the better working memory performance we maintain. Psychologist Oscar Yvarra, a University of Michigan researcher, concludes from his research that encouraging children to develop social skills will help them improve their intellectual skills. In the workplace, employees who are encouraged to take time out of their work routine to socialize are more effective workers.

How wise we are when we realize the gift that others are in our life and the blessing we can be for others. When we stand together and interact with each other, we create life-giving bonds that energize us and give meaning to our journey.

An old African king gathered his people and gave them a short, sturdy stick. The king instructed them to break the stick. With little effort, they all snapped their sticks in half. "This is how it is when a soul is alone without anyone. It can be easily broken."

The king next gave everyone another stick and said, "This is how I would like you to live after I pass. Put your sticks together in bundles of twos and threes. Now, break these bundles in half."

The people surrounding the king followed his instructions and tried to break the bundles. But they failed.

"No one can break the sticks when there are two or more in a bundle," the king said. "We are strong when we stand with another soul. When we are with another, we cannot be broken."

Recently, I was on a Hawaiian Airlines flight from Honolulu to Kauai and then to Maui. The clouds looked like cotton candy. The ocean below gave the clouds a beautiful blue shade. The sun was just beginning to set. Above the clouds there was a beautiful pink/orange blanket. What a breathtaking view. How can someone not believe in God, I thought? Who else could have orchestrated such a magnificent picture?

Arriving on Kauai, I was immediately welcomed with the aloha spirit. A lei of beautiful flowers was given to me and I was gifted with the aroma of ginger and plumeria for the entire day. The school faculty to whom I was lecturing only had a morning session, so I had another gift: interacting with students, who were being dismissed at 12:30 p.m., thus enabling an afternoon in-service for the faculty. The early dismissal caused some confusion. Many of the kindergarten children wandered around teary-eyed, saying that no one was there to pick them up; they were afraid of being abandoned. I took on the role of "aide" and brought children to the office, where they could telephone their parents. These stressful minutes are like hours to a five-year-old. The fear of being left behind needed to be replaced with reassurance.

I brought two kindergarten children into the office at the same time. Both had beautiful blue-grey eyes. They were almost identical and so I assumed they were brother and sister. I asked them if they were related and both children shook their heads "no." I continued my conversation with them, saying that I thought they were siblings because they had identical eyes. Immediately, they looked at each other's face. There was a Hawaiian teacher standing nearby and she joined the conversation.

"Hawaiian people have beautiful eyes. Sister Anne is right, the two of you have beautiful eyes." This produced a magnificent smile on each child's face.

She continued, "And what color are my eyes? The little girl quickly responded, "Brown."

"Yes. And what color are her eyes?" she asked as she pointed to me.

77

The girl looked over at me and said, "Ocean color!"

How many times I have thought of that gorgeous little girl who gifted me with "ocean color" eyes.

CHAPTER 10

Transforming Moments

THE FULLNESS OF JOY IS TO BEHOLD GOD IN EVERYTHING.
—JULIAN OF NORWICH

I was the first woman to be invited to join the Albany Rotary Club. I know I was their token woman. There were 200 male club members and none of their wives cared that I was joining. As a Roman Catholic nun, I was safe! I love being a member of the Albany Rotary, which does such wonderful service for the community. Members are involved in many projects that make a difference in the lives of so many in the community—especially children.

The club meets weekly and there is always a guest presenter. The speaker could be a community leader, a CEO, a motivational person, or someone who has an inspiring message to share.

One week we arrived for the meeting to be told that the speaker, Dr. Michael Moran, was unable to be with us. There was an emergency and he had to perform surgery. So the president of the club came over and asked if I would fill in and be the speaker.

I always tell people that I never speak on anything about which I have no expertise; I never address nutrition or exercise. I figure there are many experts in those areas. Besides, the only exercise I believe in is laughter. You get all the physical benefits of exercise when you laugh. Plus, it is so much easier!

When the president asked me to talk at the luncheon meeting I, of course, said I would. What was the prearranged topic? "The Prostate: Everything you ever wanted to know and were afraid to ask." Now there are *three* things I don't speak on: nutrition, exercise, and the prostate. But humor, faith, and patience can transform any crisis into an opportunity. They can change a curse into a blessing.

One day in March I was asked to open a convention in Salt Lake City, Utah. The request had come about ten months before the date and I happily said I would go. I asked the contact person if there was any way I could do the trip in one day. She questioned if I meant that I wanted to go from Albany, New York, to Salt Lake City, Utah, and return the same day. I did! She called me back later, telling me it was possible. I would leave Albany at 6:00 a.m. and arrive in Salt Lake City by 11:00 a.m. I was speaking at noon and I could depart Salt Lake City on a 3:45 p.m. flight which would arrive in Albany at 11:30 p.m. Obviously there were time changes, but they wouldn't affect anyone else but myself. The contact person booked the flight and sent me the tickets.

The day before I was supposed to arrive, the woman called, asking where I was. I reminded her I was coming the next day. She was in a state of panic, worrying because it was winter and wondering what would happen if I couldn't get

80

there. There were 2,500 people booked for the convention and I was doing the opening keynote address. I tried to assure her I would be there and reminded her that she had arranged the trip and sent me my ticket.

The woman called back four times during the day and each time her fears and anxieties were intensified. I suggested we "believe" and "have faith" but no message was decreasing her fears. I even said a few prayers myself, hoping I wouldn't disappoint her!

The following morning I left Albany at 6:00 a.m. and arrived in Salt Lake City at 11:00 a.m. As I was getting off the plane I saw a woman holding a sign with my name on it. As I came through the door of the terminal into the waiting space I could hear a voice over the crowd chanting, "I believe. I believe. I believe."

I walked over to the woman and said, "See what happens when you have faith!"

Humor does decrease stress—if we let it.

We have daily liturgy at our provincial house—where many of our retired sisters live. Often a sister will make a donation to have a liturgy offered for someone who is ill, someone in need of prayers, or for a remembrance of a birthday or anniversary. During the recent difficult ordeal in my life to which I alluded earlier, one of the sisters gave an offering to have me remembered in one of the liturgies. The sister responsible for arranging the Masses always lists two intentions for each Mass. She scheduled my intention the same day as a memorial liturgy for a very close friend of mine—Sister Catherine Daly—who had died one month earlier.

The sister who was reading the offertory petitions read the final petition, "And for Sister Catherine Daly and Sister Anne Bryan Smollin, who are being remembered in this eucharistic celebration, let us pray to the Lord."

From the back of our very large chapel a sister who is hard of hearing, whispered, in a whisper that could be heard in the front of the chapel, "Did Sister Anne die?"

"No," an equally hard-of-hearing sister next to her responded. "She's sitting up there in the front of the chapel."

Our doorbell rang the night before Thanksgiving. I went to our front door and looked through the windowpane in the door; not seeing anyone I began walking to our back door. There was no evidence of anyone at the back door. The doorbell rang again. I returned to our front door and this time I opened the door. There on the doorstep was a child about four or five years old, holding in his arms a big turkey.

He wasted no time on a long conversation but reached out his short arms to me and delivered the turkey. He said, "This is for you because you are poor."

I took the turkey and told the youngster how grateful I was for this Thanksgiving gift and tried to make conversation with him.

"Can I eat this?"

"Oh no. Your mom has to cook it first."

He smiled and immediately left.

I returned to our kitchen holding the turkey and remembering this child's message: "This is for you because you are poor."

We are poor if we have not learned the generous giving that this little child had obviously been taught. It was evident he came only to give. He wanted nothing in return. He barely waited long enough to hear a "thank you." I was reminded of the great Christmas story, ". . . and a little child shall lead them." We can learn much from children.

[Jesus said,] "I have said these things to you so that my joy may be in you, and that your joy may be complete. 'This is my commandment, that you love one another as I have loved you.'"

—John 15:11–12

84

CHAPTER 11

Memories— Journal of the Heart

"THE CHILD WHO BROUGHT ME ONE SMALL ROSE"
I TAUGHT HIM HOW TO WRITE HIS NAME,
SOME NURSERY RHYMES, A CHILDREN'S GAME.
AND WHEN HE BROUGHT ME ONE SMALL ROSE
HE BROUGHT MORE HEAVEN THAN HE KNOWS.
FOR WOVEN WITH THE ROSE'S SCENT
HIS WORDLESS LOVE WAS ELOQUENT.
AND HE SKIPPED AWAY. BUT FOR AWHILE
I COULD NOT STIR, NOR COULD I SAY
HOW LOVE POSSESSED ME ALL THAT DAY.
—EILEEN LOMASNEY, CSJ
LIGHT FROM ANOTHER ROOM

My friend Sister Eileen Lomasney died this past year. Eileen was a poet, an artist, an author, and a woman who cherished each moment of life. Her poetry opened up the magic and spirituality of each raindrop, each leaf, each person who graced her presence. We knew her soul deeply as she touched ours with her poems. The beautiful children's books she penned were enjoyed by children of all ages. As is true when a loved one dies, we now hold her words, her books, and her poems in our hearts, endearing her memory as we reverence her life's work.

Her close friends were asked to go through her belongings and clean out her apartment. My assignment was to go through the cartons of photographs and categorize them in piles for family members, friends, and community. The other assignment I received was to go through the bags and boxes of cards—many of which had never been opened. As I held each photograph, opened each envelope, and looked at the letter or card, I was immersed in Eileen's world. It was a profound journey for me as I traveled though such personal, sacred artifacts. I saw pictures of her with her loved ones and felt like I was walking in another's intimate world. I respected each picture, realizing that it detailed her life story. It revealed Eileen's feelings and the feelings of others in the photographs. There were posed pictures and pictures that were so obviously spontaneous. There were pictures with family members that recalled for me Eileen's way of complementing the many facets of her life, bringing family and friends together. There were pictures of her wonderful, supportive friends whom she held so dear. There were photos of retreats, vacations, poetry readings, and holiday celebrations that framed her personal memories, capturing a life rich in blessings.

There were holiday cards and birthday cards, notes and letters filled with updates on the health of family members. As I opened each envelope, I looked to see who it was from, removed any contents from the envelope, and then discarded the note. I couldn't allow myself to read the inscriptions—those personal messages meant for Eileen from those who loved her.

It took days to complete these tasks. Each evening I would spend about three hours sifting through the notes and photos. At the end of the time my hands were heavy. The weight of these rich memories and messages was left in my hands. They ached as I felt both the privilege and pain of my friend's life slip through my fingers.

Memories are truly gifts. They allow us to recall loved ones and happy occasions and moments that connect us with each other. Memories keep us company and in the very act of remembering, we can often find ourselves smiling. Memories warm our hearts and keep us connected to others even when we are alone. Perhaps memories are things we hold onto so that we never have to be truly alone. We can carry good times, happy times, loved ones, funny situations, birthday parties, weddings, and surprises in our hearts and minds, and we can use these to nourish both heart and soul.

We all need *he*roes and *she*roes in our lives. These are the people we imitate and hold in high esteem. Some people idolize movie stars or sports figures. For others, it can be a favorite teacher or coach that becomes a role model. For some it may be a parent, relative, or neighbor. All of us can recall a person whom we have put on a pedestal, emulating his or her most desired qualities.

When I was growing up I idolized Althea Gibson. She was the first African-American woman ever to win the English Grand Slam Tennis Tournament, Wimbledon. I remember watching her play tennis on television and wishing I could play against her. I was convinced that I would win, of course. I read and reread her autobiography, *I've Always Wanted to Be Somebody*, for every book report that was required in high school. My English teacher

89

finally came to me one day and told me to read another book. She was tired of reading about Althea Gibson!

In December of my senior year of high school Althea Gibson was scheduled to play a tennis match in Albany, New York. I couldn't wait to attend. A few of my friends and I arrived early for the designated event to be held at the Washington Avenue Armory. The first person I met as we walked into the facility was Althea's manager. Somehow I began a conversation with this gentleman and, when I realized who he was, I told him that Althea was the only idol I ever had. I also informed him that I could beat her. He asked if I wanted to meet her and he took me into her dressing room. There, as big as life, standing in front of me was my hero. I'm not sure how tall she really was, but I thought she was a giant. She reached out to shake my hand and I remember thinking I had never felt a hand so big and so strong.

"I can beat you," I assured her.

She responded that I probably could. "Tennis is a mental game. Any sixteen-year-old that believes she could beat me probably can."

We talked for a few minutes and she told me to come on tour with her; she would work with me and, after a year, her team could determine whether I would be Wimbledon material. At the end of the evening I rushed home to pack my clothes. My mother informed me that I wasn't going anywhere until I passed English 4. That was all I needed to graduate since I had completed the other requirements for a New York State Regents diploma. The English 4 exam was given in January. This was December and that English exam was blocking my future plans. My mother wisely concluded that, if I really wanted to join

Althea Gibson when I graduated from high school, I would find a way.

The following March, Althea Gibson returned to New York's Capital Region again. This time she played a tennis match in the Troy Armory. Again, my friends and I were at the event. We had front-row seats! At the completion of the match Althea Gibson walked over to me, reached out her hand and called me by name. Needless to say, my feet didn't touch the ground all evening.

Althea Gibson was a woman who believed in herself, regardless of what the world was saying. She was an African American woman in an all white, elite world of tennis. She played the game with an intensity and focus that brought her from the streets of Harlem to the center court of Wimbledon. Althea Gibson was a shero.

Everyone feels affirmed when being recognized and acknowledged. We all need to be noticed. The scars that are left when one is unrecognized and unappreciated are deep.

91

The sister I live with runs a music school—Carondelet Music Center. Students of all ages—from birth to eighty-four years young—attend weekly music classes. Each year on the first day of the semester, I go out to the center and take pictures of the students for her. I get to see the children who won't leave their mother's side and seem so insecure in this strange place. I then return on the last day of classes and take pictures again. What changes occur: Children come into the room without a parent or caregiver, they run over to their new friends, with whom they have established rich social bonds, and their cheerful voices and joyful laughter add to the room's excitement.

One little fellow, Matthew, had been coming to the music center since he was two months old. Now he was

Live, Laugh, and

starting kindergarten. I get to interact with the parents when I take the photos and have chatted several times with Matthew's mom. She told me how much he loves music and can't wait for Monday to come so he can go to music class. She said he begins each week asking, "How many more days until music class, Mom?"

Knowing that he had begun kindergarten, I asked Matthew's mom how he liked school. She related how difficult this transition has been for him and how upsetting it is to watch. Knowing how much he loved music, she was hoping that this week, which included music class in school, might ease his adjustment. She couldn't wait to ask him about it. She said he came into the house and looked sad. When she asked him what was wrong he responded, "Nothing." She waited a bit and then decided to address school again. This time she asked how music class was.

Stripped of enthusiasm and without joy, Matthew replied, "It was okay."

She continued, "How was Dan, the Music Man?"

"He was okay," was Matthew's response.

"Well, did you like him?" asked Matthew's mom.

"I don't know. He didn't even notice me," replied Matthew.

What a sad, true story. We all need to be acknowledged.

CHAPTER 12

Heroes and Sheroes

JESUS SAID, "IF YOU BRING FORTH WHAT IS WITHIN YOU,
WHAT YOU BRING FORTH WILL SAVE YOU."
—GNOSTIC GOSPEL OF ST. THOMAS

Children often have heroes and sheroes. They often imitate others and hold people in high esteem. Some idolize movie stars or sports figures and desire to be like them. For others, there is a favorite teacher or coach or principal that becomes an exemplary model in their life. For some children it may be a parent or a relative or a next-door neighbor. All of us can recall a person whom we have put on a pedestal in the hope of emulating their desired qualities.

I have had the privilege of meeting many wonderful people. I've been introduced to political figures as well as dignitaries. I've been in the company of CEOs, COOs, and many successful business people. I've met bishops, cardinals, and religious leaders of many faiths. I have sat side-by-side with many prominent sports figures, sharing the stage with them as presenters at various conventions. In addition, there are so many prestigious therapists who have contributed to the field and with whom I have had the pleasure of association.

Irecall one time speaking at a Salt Lake City convention when former Chicago Bears running back Walter Payton, was also on the speaking roster. The two of us were having such a great time conversing with each other that we were unaware of our introductions from the stage. While out in the hall talking to one another, we were totally oblivious that the convention was beginning. He was a giant, not in height, but in the way he lived and served others.

When I was studying counseling techniques, I looked to psychotherapist Carl Rogers as my role model. His compassion and warmth were the values that came through his live demonstrations of counseling sessions at convention workshops. I remember walking out of the convention hall in Phoenix, Arizona, and seeing Carl Rogers with Virginia Satir, another giant in the field. When Carl Rogers held the door open for me, I thanked him, and what I remember most was his graciousness. These moments are special memories.

So often the "wonderful," "influential" people we meet are people we see every day. Not big-name people but people who stand for dignity, valuing life itself.

I recently attended the funeral and burial of a dear friend, Miriam Cavanaugh. Miriam is the mother of Janet, one of my best friends. Janet and I entered the Sisters of Saint Joseph together when we were both seventeen years old, sharing a friendship from the moment we met. Miriam was one of those influential people who touched other peoples' lives through her simple acceptance of them.

Many people who came to her wake took the time to tell stories about Miriam. It was wonderful to watch smiles appear on her daughters' faces and hear the sound of laughter in the funeral home. Our faith tells us she is with our God and is at peace and will not have to endure any more suffering. As consoling as that is, we, her family and friends, must still deal with the loss of this great woman. We are human and we are left with the feeling of emptiness and grief.

During this sad time I watched how family members were supportive of each other. The grandchildren tried to be there and do whatever needed to be done, while the great-grandchildren were very quiet. One great-grandchild sadly related, the minute she saw me, "*My* Mimi died." Her big brown eyes had tears in them as she kept looking at "Mimi" who wasn't sitting up, talking, and laughing. Deep down, this four-year-old knew she wasn't really there.

All of this made me think about my own mother. Mom is *always* there and open to new opportunities and challenges. She's a loyal, faithful person. The week before she died Miriam asked to see her friend, my mom. I will always remember my mom and Janet's mom sitting next to each other on the couch, holding hands, talking, and reminiscing for the last time.

My mother never passes up an opportunity to tell us how proud of us she is. She is a woman of deep faith who has learned how to pray always, all ways. She keeps herself interested in the world we live in by keeping herself knowledgeable regarding the news. And the Yankees! If only they knew what a devoted fan they have in her. She quotes batting averages and has her calendar marked with the times they are playing and the score of each game.

Mom also has learned the importance in being of service to others. She is a friendly visitor to many sisters at our provincial house. Her weekly visits bring companionship and joy to our retired and sick sisters. Many of the sisters are even younger than my mother, but it would be hard to guess that. She stays young and alive.

The real heroes and sheroes are not people who appear on television or who get honored with awards but are the Moms and Miriams of the world. They are the people who gift us with their presence, bring smiles to our faces, and spend time in companionship. They are the ones who, from day to day, model lives that make us healthier, happier, and holier people because we know them.

CHAPTER 13

Living Through Things

WE HOLD ON TO AND TAKE CARE OF WHAT WE LOVE AND WHAT LOVES US.

Sometimes when we feel overwhelmed we just want to give it all up. A principal of a school was telling me how hard it is trying to stay on top of things. There are teachers, students, and parents, as well as regulations from school offices and state education departments. She said it was hard to find the value in what she was doing day after day. As we talked about it, she said she hated to go into the faculty room any more. It used to be a gathering place where teachers would come together and one could hear the sound of laughter coming from the room all the way down the hallway. Now, however, it's a place where the faculty gathers to complain about the students and all that has to be done. It's so negative!

What we need to do is look for what is life-giving. Will we find it in the positive energy of laughter or in the negative messages of complaint? Negativity not only creates an uncomfortable atmosphere but it also drains life out of any institution. The worst part is it becomes contagious. It often leads to "who has the worst story to tell" or "who can top this with a horrible event." There is no hope after awhile.

Someone once told me that the longer you complain the longer God lets you live! Maybe that's why the saying exists: "Only the good die young!"

We stay stuck in these ruts and feed off of each other and often forget the fact that we have the ability to make a choice and the power to turn things around. Today doesn't have to be a photocopy of yesterday. Tomorrow has the potential of being filled with wonders and blessings and surprises.

All professions have difficult moments that have to be worked through. Life is not a bed of roses and even a person with a positive attitude will find that it doesn't mean seeing life through rose-colored glasses. It means making the choice to find options to deal with whatever is in front of us.

I have a friend who teaches a sixth-grade class of mentally challenged children. Every year her class puts on a play, and the students can't wait to get into sixth grade so they can be on the stage and act in the play. She was telling me about a play where the main character was God. The script called for "God" to stop in the middle of the play and ask the audience if there were any questions. She was hoping the audience would be kind to these children and not pose any question at all. It was obvious the students were serious about their roles and doing their very best. At the appropriate time "God" stopped and asked if there were any questions. A woman in the front row raised her hand and asked, "Tell me, why is there so much suffering in the world?" My friend expressed her feelings of anger and wondered why anyone would pose such a difficult question to this student. But God was with "God" and the student looked out at the audience and replied, "Look, I made the sky blue and the grass green. Now you have to do your part."

By trusting ourselves, and each other, we can be free to find these life-giving moments that come into our lives daily. "God" is in all of us. Finding that energy involves trusting who we are and living fully the moment that lies in front of us.

For years I have facilitated an adolescent therapy group. It is always the highlight of my week. Adolescents are so real, so honest. They don't have the masks adults have learned to wear. Once the adolescent trusts, there are few fears they would hesitate to state.

One of these adolescent sessions was with a group of girls aged 14 to 17 who have had babies. They were now living in a group facility where they could learn parenting skills while also completing their high school educations. The sessions were held weekly and as the girls grew more open and verbal in the group it was evident they began to trust much more. Even though they lived together, the group became the place where issues would be brought up and confrontations were honest and direct. Few words were spared or weighed during that group time.

For about seven sessions, the group membership was stable. Then a new girl came to live at the residence and consequently came to the group sessions with the other girls. She sat very quietly but was stunned as she listened to the issues the girls had "saved up" to talk about in the session. Because she was new to the group, I tried to gently include her. She didn't know me or the other girls yet; I needed some time to develop a trust level with her and between us.

The second week the new member was in the group, she arrived with a few of the girls a bit early. They were chatting as they waited for the rest of the group members to arrive. The new girl turned to me and said, "Are you married?"

Her friend seated next to her answered for me, "No, she can't get married; she's a sister."

The newest member turned to me and responded, "Oh, I didn't know that. I'm not Catholic."

She continued her questioning immediately, asking me, "Do you have a boyfriend?"

Again her roommate responded, "She can't have a boyfriend. She's a nun."

Again she said, "Oh, I didn't know. I'm not Catholic."

However, this didn't stop her. "Do you have any children?"

"She can't have children. She's a nun."

"Oh, I didn't know. I'm not Catholic."

Now she looked totally confused. Since the conversation was between the two girls who resided together I wasn't sure where we were going with this issue. The two girls continued their conversation while I listened.

"What does she do for . . . for . . . you know, what does she do for sex?"

"She can't have sex. She has a vow. Anyway, she is thirty-five years old and they didn't do it back then."

I was only a listener. I certainly didn't want to have to clarify my age! At this point in the conversation, the rest of the girls came into the room. It wasn't until the end of the session that the newest member talked directly to me.

"The girls really like you. They trust you. They talk about coming to group and save certain things to talk about in the group. You're a nice person. You should have someone to go home to each night who is there only for you."

This comment opened up one of the best discussions I've ever had on commitment. I talked about how we make choices and how we must have boundaries in our lives. What I remember most about the discussion was this central awareness: Commitment is something which holds responsibilities. One of the young adolescent mothers said, "Wow! It's like when you make a commitment you gotta live it right forever."

101

"Blessed are the poor in spirit, for theirs is the kingdom of heaven. Blessed are those who mourn, for they will be comforted. Blessed are the meek, for they will inherit the earth. Blessed are those who hunger and thirst for righteousness, for they will be filled. Blessed are the merciful, for they will receive mercy. Blessed are the pure in heart, for they will see God. Blessed are the peacemakers, for they will be called children of God. Blessed are those who are persecuted for righteousness' sake, for theirs is the kingdom of heaven. Blessed are you when people revile you and persecute you and utter all kinds of evil against you falsely on my account. Rejoice and be glad, for your reward is great in heaven, for in the same way they persecuted the prophets who were before you."

—Matthew 5:3–12

102

CHAPTER 14

Caring for Ourselves

WHAT LIES BEHIND US AND WHAT LIES BEFORE US ARE TINY MATTERS COMPARED TO WHAT LIES WITHIN US.
—RALPH WALDO EMERSON

Why is it that we hesitate to take care of ourselves? We don't have time to relax. We don't have time to just be in someone else's company. We don't know how to sit and be still. Silence would be deafening to many. Everyone needs a hobby or an interest. We all need something we can do just for ourselves. If we don't, we begin to resent the fact that everyone else has an interest while we take care of everyone else except ourselves. As we take the time to do something we enjoy, we rest our minds and bodies, we energize our hearts and souls.

These essential things bring balance into our life. These are the stress reducers that give us a bit of respite from the tensions and pressures that exist in each day. These are the gifts that let us have breaks so we can go back to whatever reality we are facing in our life at that time. Our jobs still get done. We even become more responsible because we return with new vigor and new insights.

Photography is my gift to myself. I get lost with my camera and take the time to see the world through the lens. It gives me a new perspective. It stretches my creativity. It teaches me that there are many ways I can look at the same thing. By shifting the focus a fraction of an inch I can change the picture. By turning the camera from horizontal to vertical a whole new perspective is viewed. I can decide what will be the focal point of the photo.

Not to take time and enjoy my camera and explore what new photos I can produce would almost be violating my *self*. I would be saying that I'm not important enough to enjoy this. I would focus on "shoulds," such as "I should be working harder" or "I shouldn't be wasting time on a hobby."

The images I can create with my camera are endless. It's just not the finished photo that is produced but also the lower blood pressure, the relaxing muscles, the body muscles used, the challenge to the mind, and the laughter and smiles that result because I've treated my whole being to this wonderful experience. Moments like this enable us to experience wholeness. We grow physically, mentally, emotionally, and spiritually as we give ourselves the right to relax a bit and absorb life in the moment.

The interesting part of relaxing is that it doesn't have to cost any money. We could find ourselves sitting in a beautiful park enjoying the beauty of the flowers or just "people gazing." Perhaps it might be writing in a journal and recalling wonderful memories that bring a smile to our face even while we are recording them. It could be as simple as listening to Johnny Mathis sing a favorite song just to us.

Recently, Johnny Mathis was in Albany, New York, for an evening performance. I just happened to be in the parking lot of the hotel where he was staying and ran into him the evening before the scheduled performance. I even had a picture taken of us together. My proof we met! When I asked him if he was going to sing the concert the following evening just for me, he replied, "Of course!"

A group of us treated ourselves to a nostalgic evening and attended the concert. What a wonderful time we had. I didn't even mind that the Palace Theater was filled to capacity; I was willing to share Johnny Mathis singing all those wonderful old tunes that hold so many memories for all of us. I knew he was singing only to me!

As he walked off the stage he saw me and waved—further proof he sang only to me! The best part was that all my friends in the audience saw it! So many commented to me about it. I absolutely loved it. I am sure Johnny Mathis tells everyone the same thing, "I'll sing just for you." But that night he did it for me.

It's moments like this that we enjoy and are able to recall years later. These are occasions that prevent us from taking ourselves too seriously. Mark Twain reminded us that humans were "made at the end of the week's work, when God was tired." We are supposed to enjoy life and the moments that gift us with our memories. Positive memories warm our hearts and are gifts we can share with others. Again, it is the connectedness with each other that aids us in living fully. We have the opportunity to laugh a bit more and share our stories and, thus, the loneliness is decreased. We don't have to feel alone; we can find ourselves in communion with each other. We feed each other not only nourishment from our tables but also sustenance in our shared lives.

From these moments we find that rituals are established. Rituals are wonderful activities that bring connection and security—everyday rituals like at meals and bedtime and special celebrations such as birthdays, Mother's Day, and Valentine's Day. We have rituals that help us celebrate community: weddings, funerals, and graduations establish the connectedness that allow us to feel like we belong.

There are times that we establish our own rituals and behaviors that help us fill a need. J. M. Barrie, the author of *Peter Pan*, lived with a mother who suffered from depression. His older brother had died and young James's mother withdrew into her own world. James would go into her room each day and tell her stories, hoping to get her attention. James later became an author, and in 1904 he wrote *Peter Pan: The Boy Who Would Not Grow Up*. It was the daily storytelling to his mother that helped him develop the creative side of his personality.

Religions have a lot of rituals which give a sense of security and belonging to the members. Worshipers use holy water, burn incense, light candles, sing songs—all of these rituals help us make sensory connections that enable us to feel like we belong. We bless ourselves, bow, sit, and stand at appropriate times. We recite prayers from memory and have our favorite saints we invoke in times of need.

This also happens in families and with our friends. We have rituals that define our relationships. We send cards for holidays and special days. We have songs that we sing when we come together. We have holiday rituals: whose house we eat Christmas dinner at; who sets the table, cooks the meal, decorates the house, etc. These are the things that make us feel like we belong and are connected.

An old Sufi tale relates how the wise fool Nasrudin used to stand in the street on market days to be pointed out as an idiot. No matter how often people offered him a large and a small coin, he always chose the smaller piece.

One day, a kindly man, obviously trying to help Nasrudin, said to him, "Nasrudin, you should take the bigger coin. Then you will have more money and people will no longer be able to make a laughingstock of you."

"That might be true," said Nasrudin, "but if I take the larger coin, people will stop offering me money to prove I am more idiotic than they are. Then I would have no money at all."

109

CHAPTER 15

You're in Charge

AT BIRTH OUR DIVINE POTENTIAL IS FOLDED UP IN US LIKE A TENT. IT IS
LIFE'S PURPOSE TO UNFOLD THAT TENT.
—HILDEGARD OF BINGEN

It has been proven that the first thought we have each day when we awake influences our day. If we get up and immediately think, "Oh, I'm so tired; I wish I could stay in bed all day; I'm just exhausted," this will be the attitude that creates our mood for the day. If we get up and immediately think, "Great; a new day; it's wonderful to be alive," then we hold the positive feeling and that's the way the day will go.

We can teach ourselves little techniques like that to create a healthier mental attitude. We can start each day by smiling. It's a gift we'll give back to ourselves. Research indicates that facial expressions, real or imagined, can change a person's mood. So to decide to smile, whether we feel like it or not, could be the first step in being more positive throughout the day. After all, God gave us our faces, but we make our expressions.

So often people judge themselves by looking at others. We see others doing important things, but we judge our lives as very ordinary. No awards, no medals, no buildings named after us, no honorary doctorate degrees—just day after day trying, at times, to survive. Thoughts and judgments like these can cause discouragement. People get anxious and depressed and even lose hope. Life can become humdrum and routine.

Everyone, at one time or another, questions whether the right choices were made. What might have been? What else is there? What am I really meant to be doing with my life? Should I change jobs or directions or a relationship before it's too late? Have I done something worthwhile with my life?

I wish we were forced to walk through life with a mirror in front of us. We would be forced to look at that person and see "who" the person is and "what" she does. We could learn to look pleasant and happy and even alive. We would be able to see the good works we do and maybe, just maybe, grow in appreciation of those deeds. Macrina Wiederkehr wrote, "O God, help me to believe the truth about myself, no matter how beautiful."

We are who we are. I am me. Just me. You are you. Just you. Being just me to the best of my ability is really what counts. Using the gifts I have and sharing my talents are what matters. We just have to become comfortable with the person we see in the mirror and learn to love and value what we see. We don't have to measure who we are or evaluate who we are by matching ourselves against another. Our giftedness is unique.

As we acknowledge and own our gifts, we strive to be more connected with others. We want to be more balanced people and we aren't content with just surviving or being passive. Carl Jung reminds us, "We can change only that which we have accepted." So, in accepting ourselves we see other ways to challenge ourselves and grow more deeply.

When we evidence a spirit of joy and hope, our perceptions change. We experience a lightness. Everything is not black-and-white. Things aren't right and wrong. Our energy level is higher. Our desire to be healthy, whole people nudges us to live fully each moment. We tend to be more responsible.

There's a great story about a woman who dreamed she found God standing behind a counter. God greeted her and told her she could have anything her heart desired. She just needed to wish for it.

The woman didn't hesitate in making her wish. She asked for "happiness, love, and wisdom."

God looked at her and said, "I don't think you understand. I can give you only seeds. Whether they become flowers is up to you."

All of us have been blessed with seeds. What we do with them is up to us. But we can't do anything with them if we don't first acknowledge that we have them. We have to do our part.

113

There was a man who really wanted to win the lottery. He prayed, "God, let me win the lottery." The next week he prayed louder, "God, let me win the lottery." Six months later on his hands and knees he raised his eyes toward heaven and prayed, "God, let me win the lottery. If I could win the lottery my family would have everything they need." And from heaven he heard a voice say, "It would be helpful if you bought a ticket."

When we have humor in our lives we are able to do our part. We relax more and are open to more opportunities. Humor keeps us in control of ourselves. When difficulties are defining our moments or others are trying to control us, our sense of humor will help us control ourselves.

Live, Laugh, and

Then the laughter we share with others will help us deal with these difficult situations. Laughter is like a medication: it keeps us light-hearted; it also keeps us connected with others.

When this laughter and humor are present, we find ourselves able to tackle any difficult obstacle. Humor has its basis in the individual and is manifested in laughter. This is what fuels relationships; this is what connects us to each other.

Humor, faith, and patience are required to turn any curse into a blessing. They also aid us in accepting ourselves and each other.

Do not give yourself over to sorrow,

and do not distress yourself deliberately.

A joyful heart is life itself,

and rejoicing lengthens one's life span.

Indulge yourself and take comfort,

and remove sorrow far from you,

for sorrow has destroyed many,

and no advantage ever comes from it.

Jealousy and anger shorten life,

and anxiety brings on premature old age.

Those who are cheerful and merry at table

will benefit from their food.

—Sirach 30:21-25

CHAPTER 16

Twenty-Six Ways to Be Happy, Holy, and Wise

YOUR TASK
TO BUILD A BETTER WORLD, SAID GOD.
I ANSWERED: HOW?
THE WORLD IS SUCH A LARGE, VAST PLACE
SO COMPLICATED NOW
AND I, SO SMALL AND USELESS AM.
THERE'S NOTHING I CAN DO.
BUT GOD IN HIS GREAT WISDOM SAID:
JUST BUILD A BETTER YOU.
—ANONYMOUS

Accept each new day as a gift.
Believe in your goodness and the goodness of others.
Cheer for others and their successes.
Don't ever give up.
Every moment is a gift for you—live it.
Forgive others and yourself.
Give thanks for all your blessings daily.
Have faith.
Invite others to share moments with you.
Join groups and be involved.
Keep in touch with those you love.

Laugh, laugh, and laugh some more.
Make some mistakes daily—on purpose.
Never judge—give others the benefit of the doubt.
Offer to share your time and talents.
Praise the good works of others.
Quit worrying.
Relax and rest and live each day fully.
Say nice things to and about others.
Take time to play.
Understand that everything won't be perfect.
Value what you have.
Wish for the stars.
X-plain things when necessary.
You are important; don't forget that.
Zap life into everything.

CHAPTER 17

The Challenge: Joy, Laughter, Humor

THE GLORY OF GOD IS A PERSON FULLY ALIVE.
—ST. IRENAEUS

It's one thing to say this is how it should be—to find joy, laughter, and humor in our daily life—but it is another thing to know that this is what we are called and challenged to do. We are called to be radical people—to live a radical lifestyle in a starving, hungry world filled with materialism, violence, and injustices. If we want to be radical we must do just that—"go back to the root." The word radical comes from the Latin word *radix*, which means "more of the root." The root of our very existence is our God.

The scriptures document the call to live fundamentally active, positive lives. As Christians, we must hear that call. In the Old Testament there are fifty-seven references to laughter and twenty-seven recognized forms of humor; in the New Testament there are 287 references to such terms as joy, delight, gladness, laughter, and rejoicing.

The word "laugh" appears in the Bible for the first time in Genesis 17:17. God told Abraham, who was 100 years old, that his ninety-year-old wife Sarah would give birth to a son. "Then Abraham fell on his face and laughed, and said to himself, 'Can a child be born to a man who is a hundred years old? Can Sarah, who is ninety years old, bear a child?'"

In Matthew 5, Jesus' first sermon, the Beatitudes, spoke of the joy and delight that is promised to all who live this radical challenge. The word blessed also means "blissfully happy or contented." The Beatitudes end on a high note of joy: "Rejoice and be glad, for your reward is great in heaven" (Matthew 5:12).

Jesus spoke of celebration, joy, gladness, and rejoicing over and over again. He used everyday examples to teach people: that they might learn from him, hear his message, and know that joy and celebration must be part of our everyday life.

The parable of the prodigal son, illustrating the father's joy at seeing his "lost son" still a long way off, is quite poignant. "He ran and put his arms around him and kissed him." (Luke 15:20b) The father immediately made plans to celebrate: "And get the fatted calf and kill it, and let us eat and celebrate; for this son of mine was dead and is alive again; he was lost and is found!" And they began to celebrate" (Luke 15:23–24). Again, we are challenged to commemorate the fragile moments of our humanity. We need to pause, take notice of, and delight in everyday moments that offer opportunities to find joy and to celebrate our common humanity.

Jesus reminded us, in the parable of the lost sheep, that we must take time to celebrate and rejoice in our precious, yet fragile, human nature: 'Just so, I tell you, there will be more joy in heaven over one sinner who repents than over ninety-nine righteous persons who need no repentance'" (Luke 15:7).

Jesus laughs. Jesus celebrates and rejoices. Jesus delights in all things. Shouldn't the people? The Bible is a blueprint of how to find joy in our daily life. All we need to do is follow it.

Anne Bryan Smollin, C.S.J., is an international lecturer on wellness and spirituality. An educator and therapist, she holds a Ph.D. in Counseling from Walden University in Florida and is presently Executive Director of the Counseling for Laity center in Albany, New York. She is also the author of *Tickle Your Soul* (Sorin Books, 1999) and *God Knows You're Stressed* (Sorin Books, 2001).

ENRICHING SPIRIT AND SOUL

TICKLE YOUR SOUL
Live Well, Love Much, Laugh Often
ANNE BRYAN SMOLLIN

Enables readers to "wrinkle their faces with smiles" and avoid "drying up their souls like prunes."
Tickle Your Soul delivers joy, health, and wellness.
ISBN: 1-893732-00-2 / 160 pages / $12.95   Sorin Books

GOD KNOWS YOU'RE STRESSED
Simple Ways to Restore Your Balance
ANNE BRYAN SMOLLIN

You *can* manage your stress, and this book will show you how. Filled with thoughtful insights, practical suggestions, and the shared stories of others.
ISBN: 1-893732-35-5 / 160 pages / $11.95   Sorin Books

SACRED NECESSITIES
Gifts for Living with Passion, Purpose, and Grace
TERRY HERSHEY

Experience and practice some of life's sacred necessities: amazement, sanctuary, stillness, grace, simplicity, resilience and friendship. This is not a prescription for the good life; rather, it is a gentle nudge to live with an open heart and a willing spirit.
ISBN: 1-893732-93-2 / 192 pages / $14.95   Sorin Books

SPARKS OF THE DIVINE
Finding Inspiration in Our Everyday World
DREW LEDER

These lively reflections help us uncover the sacred dimension to our world, to look outward and discover a spark of the divine in everyday objects, activities, and experiences.
ISBN: 1-893732-81-9 / 256 pages / $14.95   Sorin Books

Available at your bookstore, online retailers, or from **ave maria press** at
www.avemariapress.com or 1-800-282-1865. Prices and availablity subject to change.

Keycode: FØSØ1Ø6ØØØØ